Andrea Oakley's

Explore!

Artistic Animal Encounters

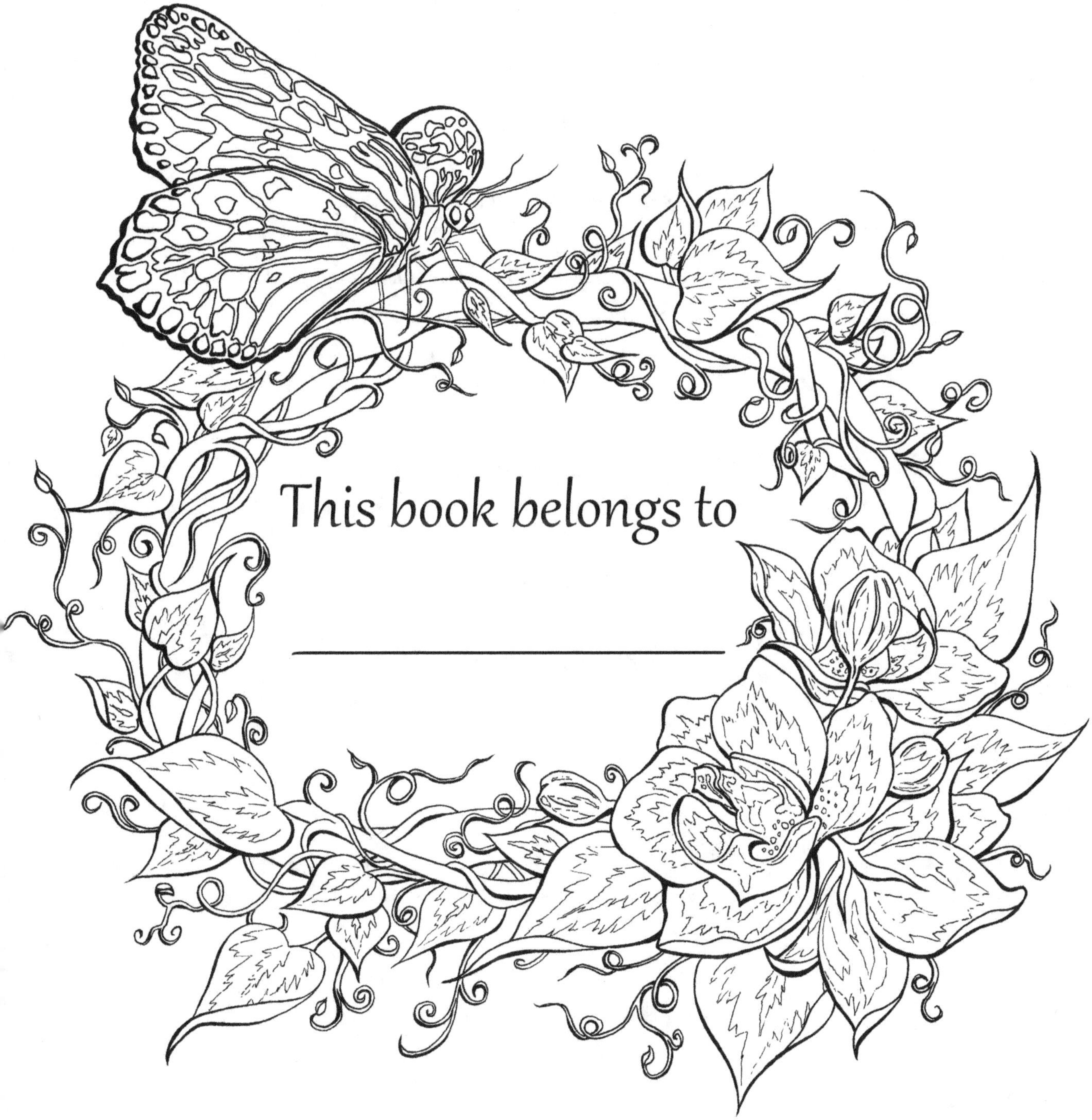

This book belongs to

_____

© 2017 Andrea Oakley

All rights reserved. No part of this book may be reproduced in any form or by any means, electronic or mechanical, including photocopy, or information storage and retrieval systems without the express written consent from the publisher.

Published in 2017 by Andrea Oakley
www.andreaspalette.com

Printed in USA

ISBN 978-1-7751795-0-4

Our journey begins...

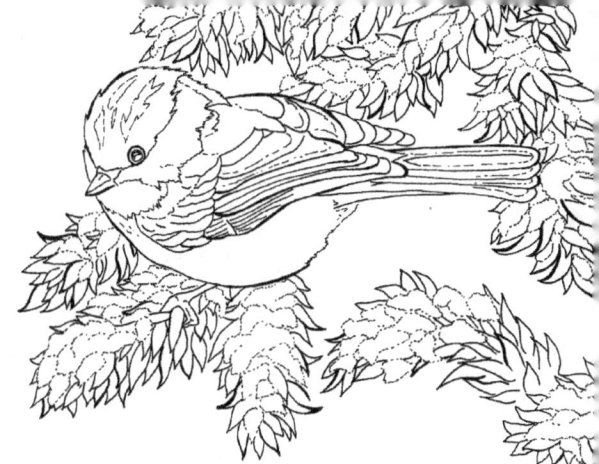

A young stallion stands strong as the wind whips around him, swirling through his gorgeous mane - the very epitome of freedom, grace and strength;

...

Elsewhere a tiny bumblebee buzzes his way through a vast field of wildflowers in his tireless quest for nectar, stopping to alight briefly on the edge of one of the delicate petals;

...

Far, far away, delightfully fuzzy panda cubs climb and play; their clumsy antics often finding them tumbling down together in the most adorably awkward way.

...

As I pick up my pens and brushes to capture a moment of time spent with any of the amazing creatures I've encountered, I always find myself drawn into their world, marvelling at their strength, their beauty, and everything that makes them unique.

With color in hand, I invite you to join me in my exploration of the fascinating animal kingdom. Get lost with me in the details of these beautiful animal encounters as you bring each one to life with stunning color!

Andrea Oakley

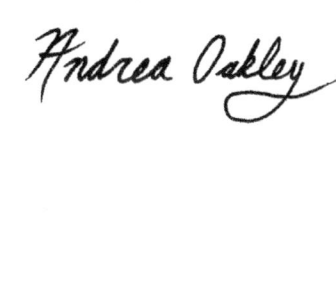

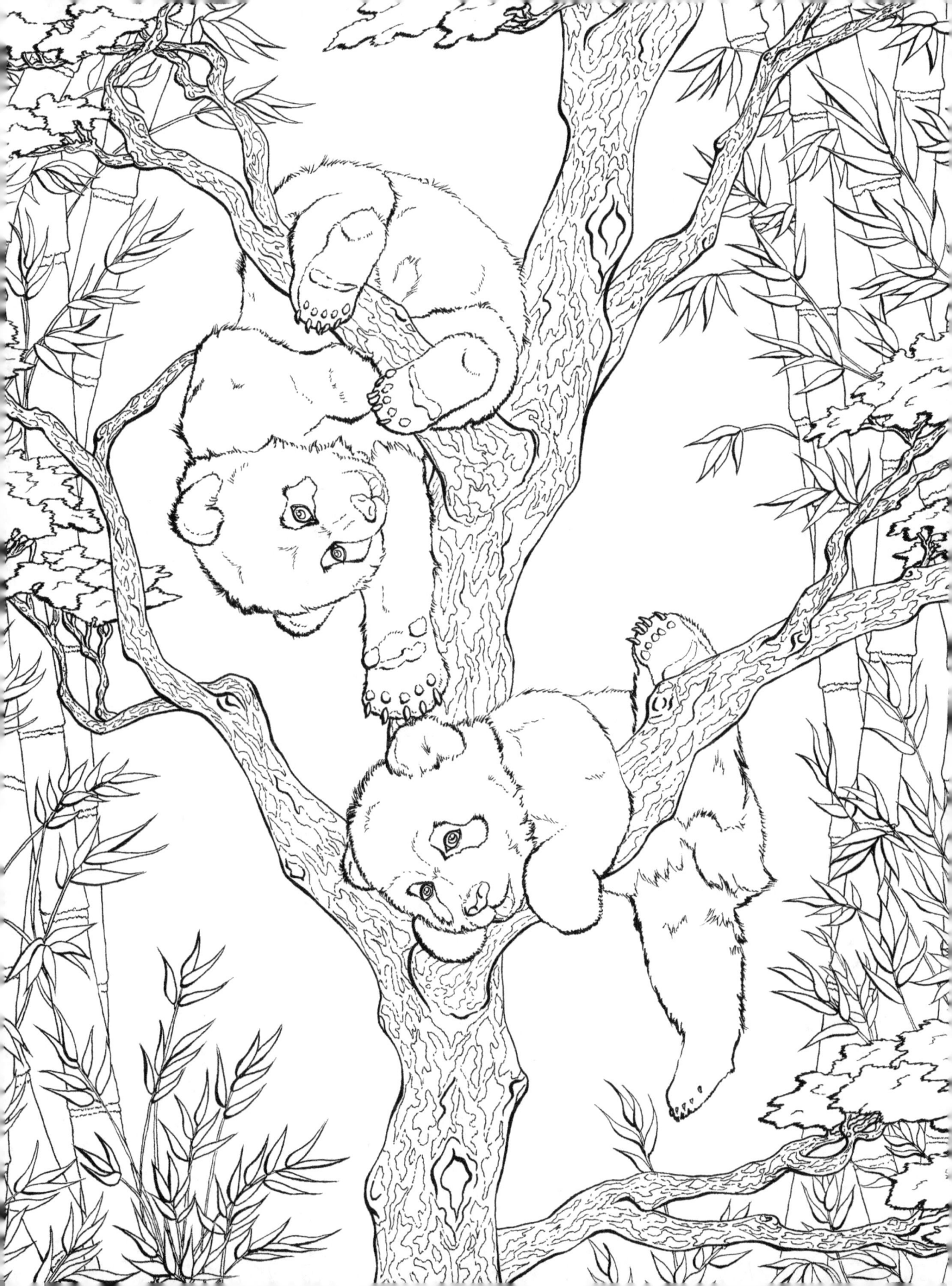

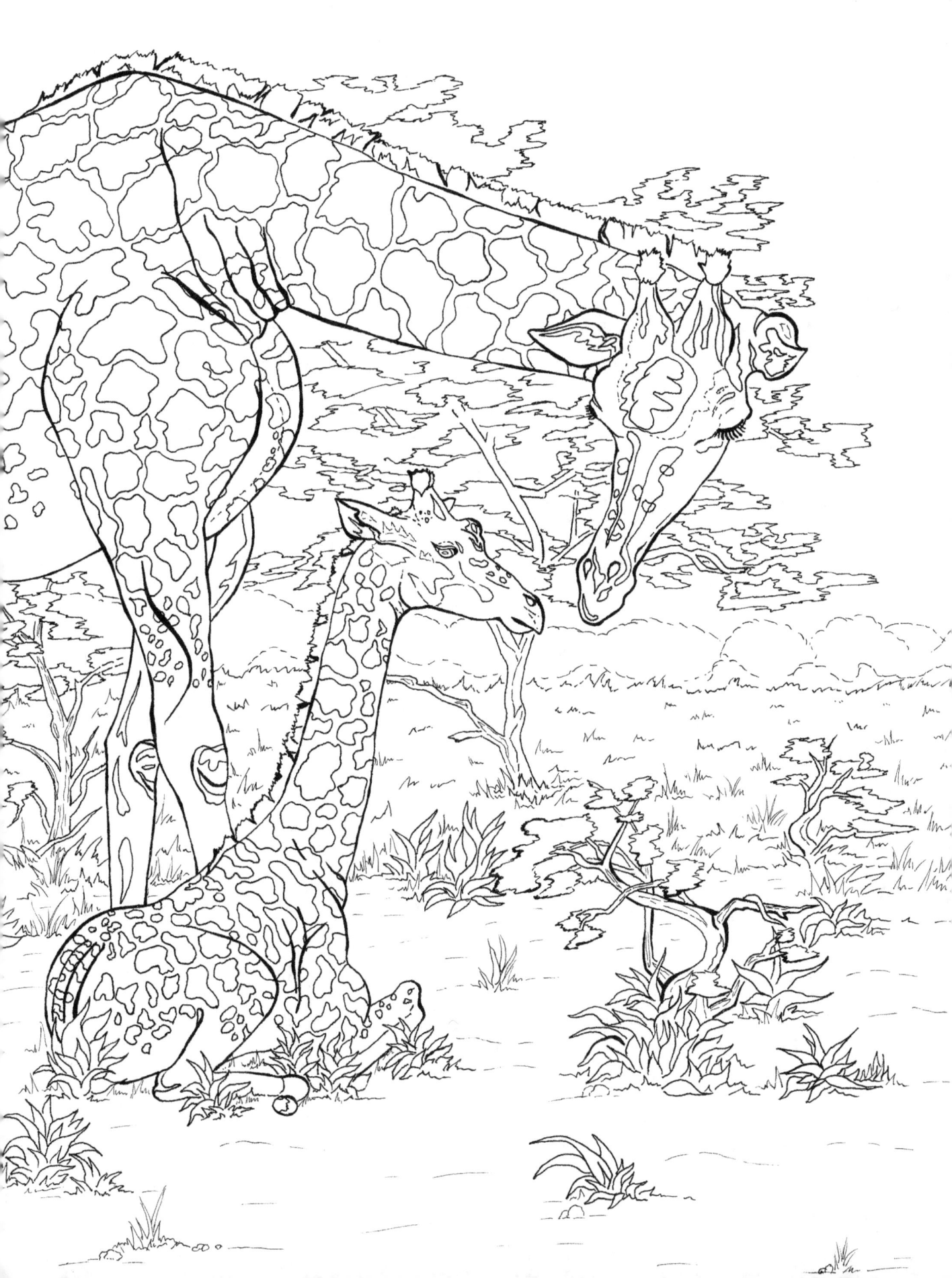

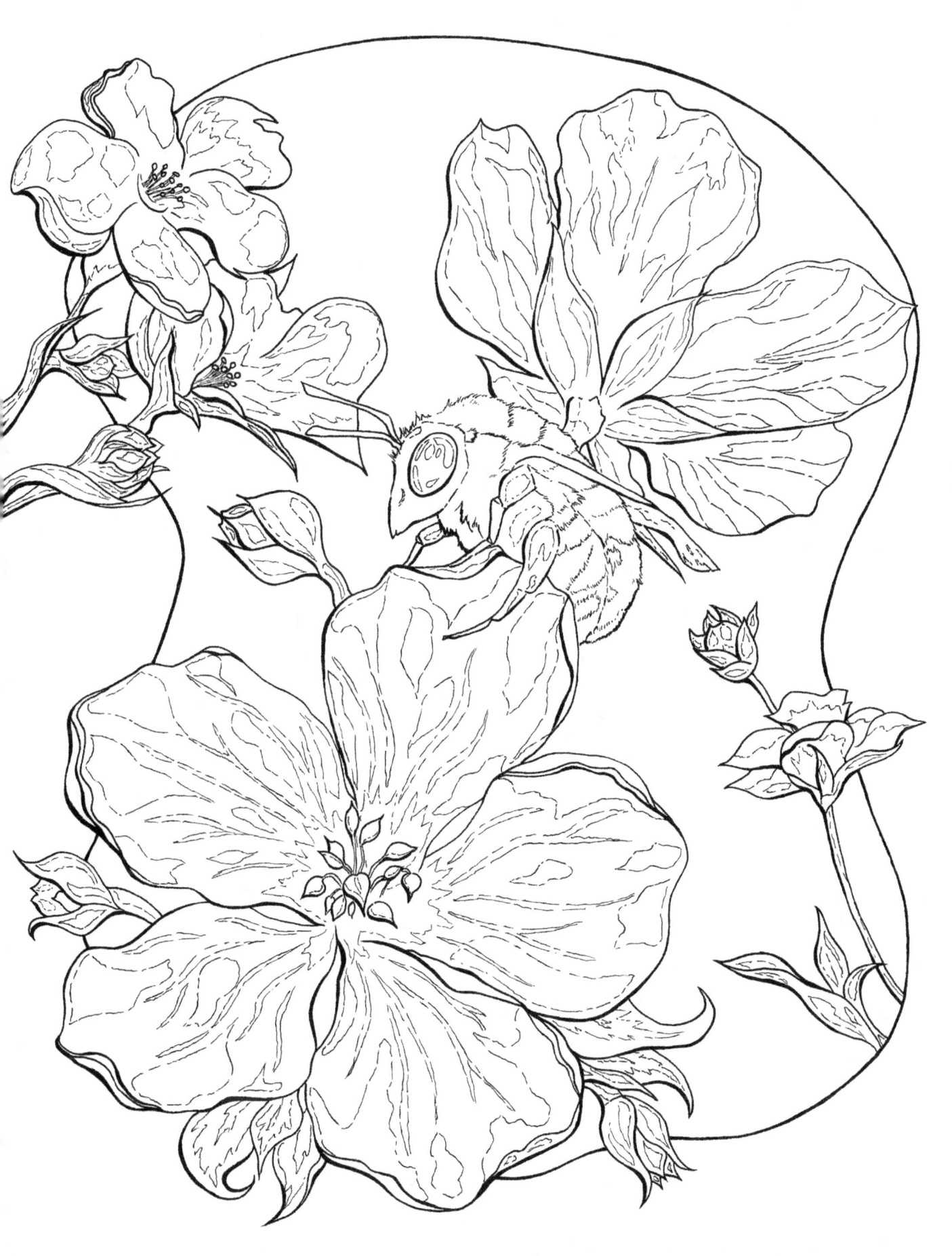

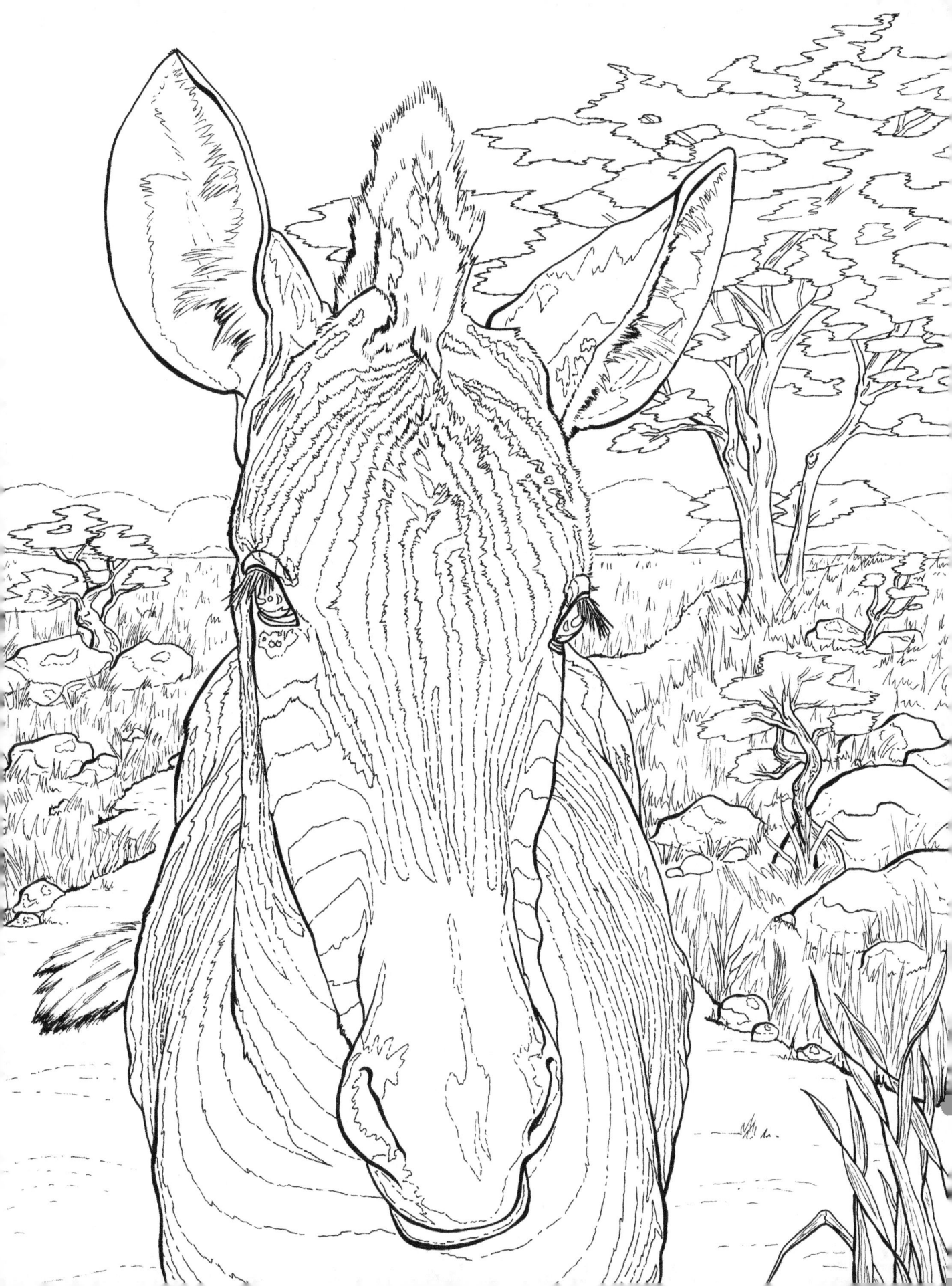

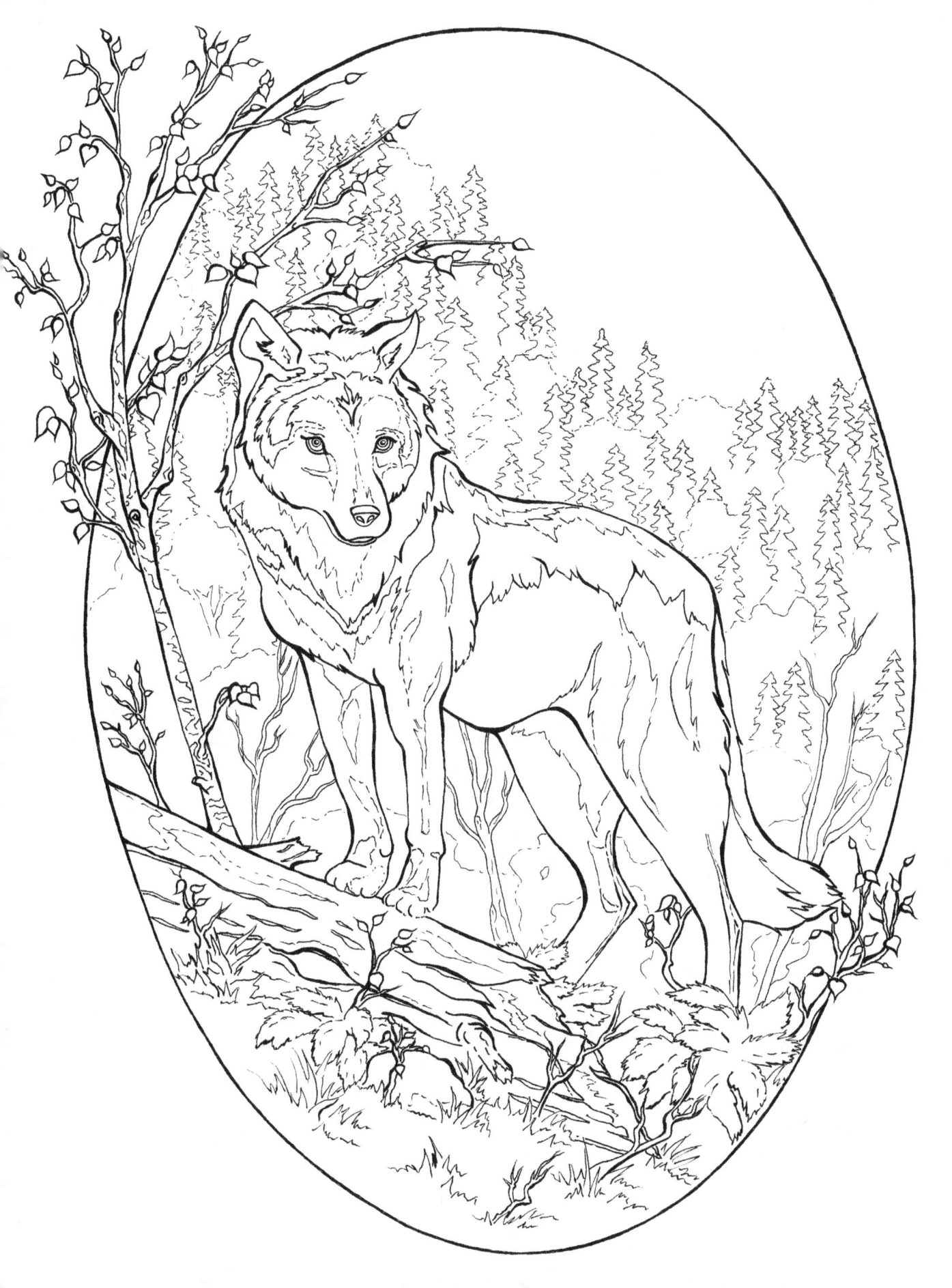

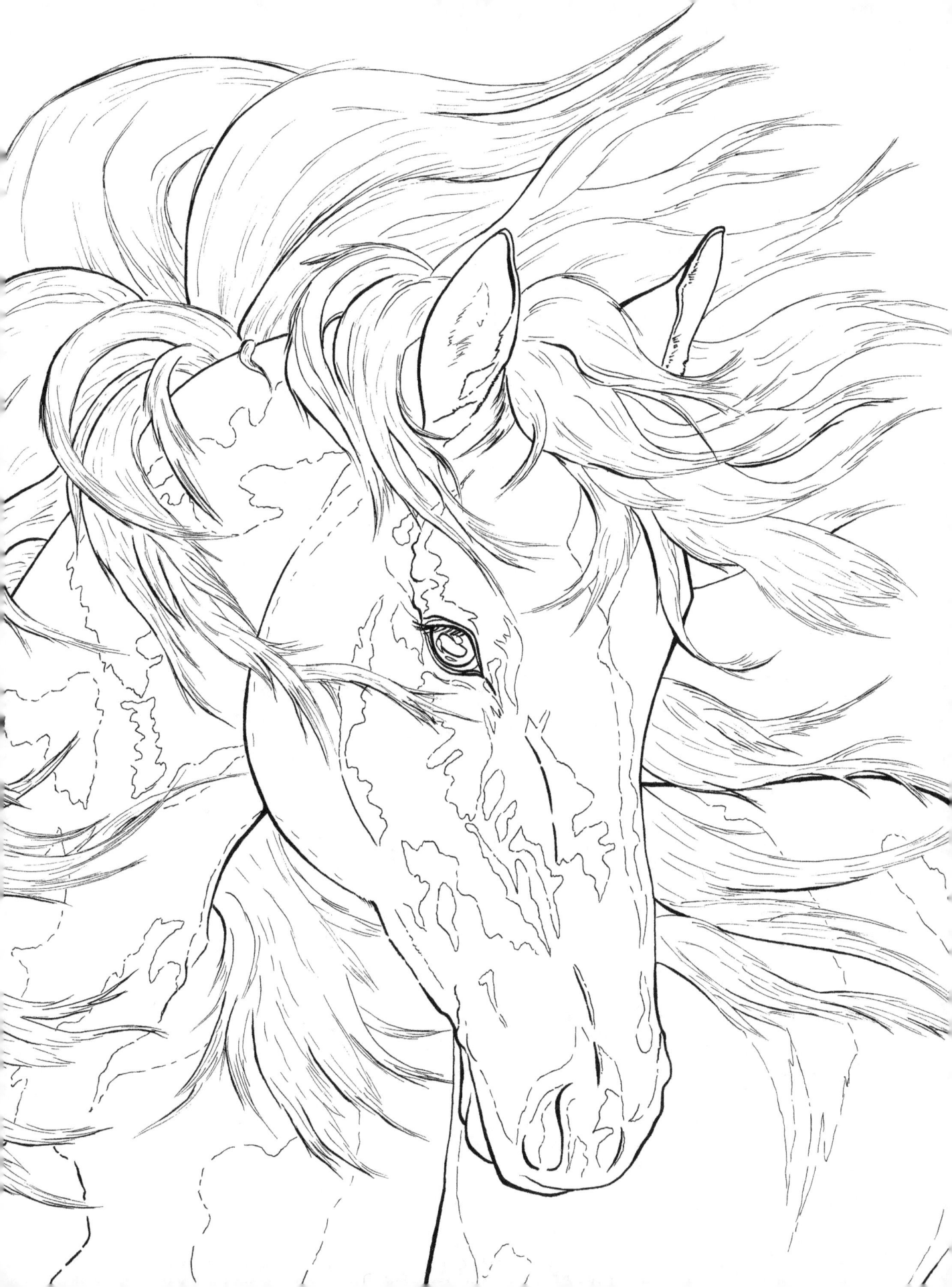

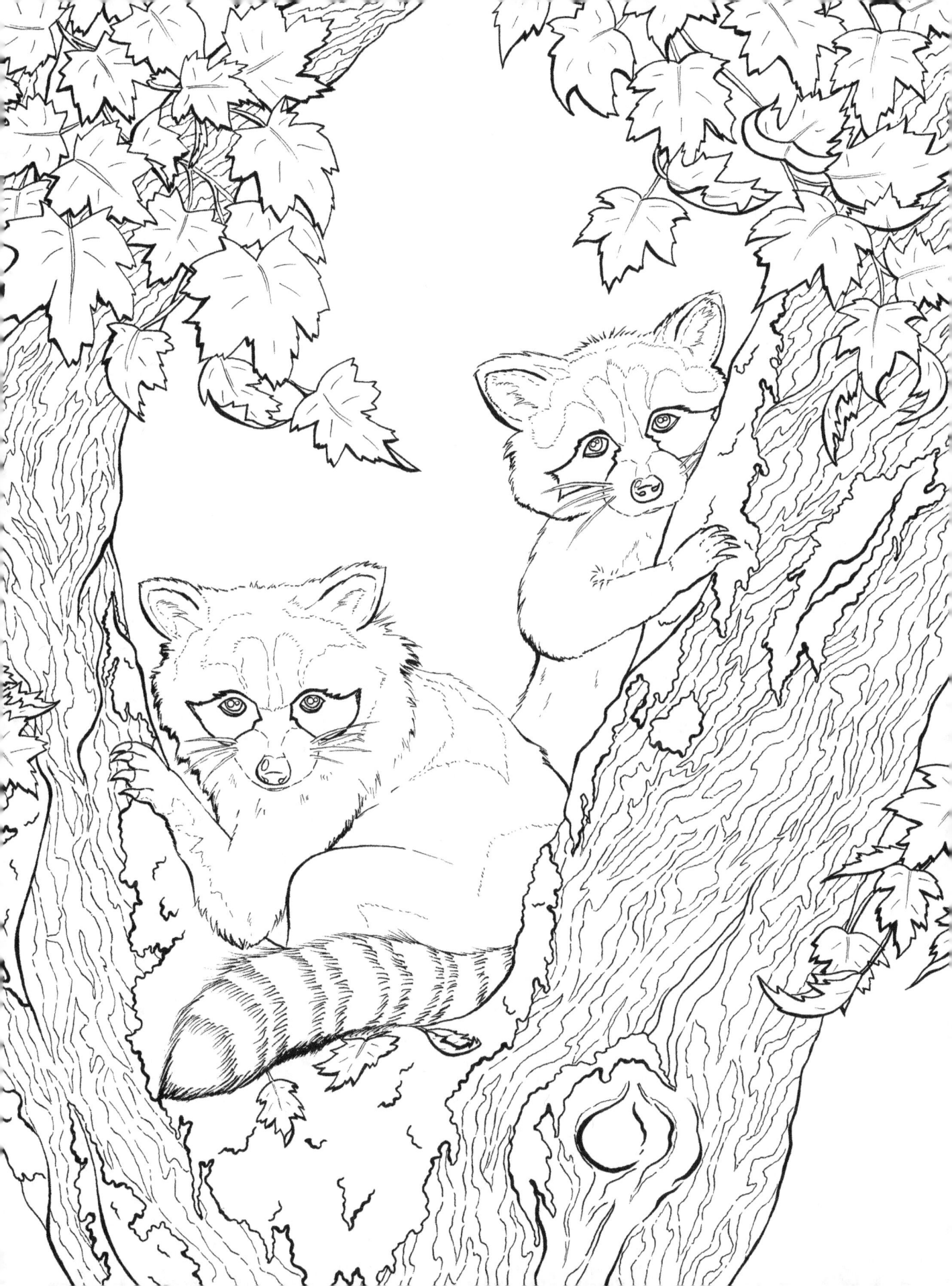

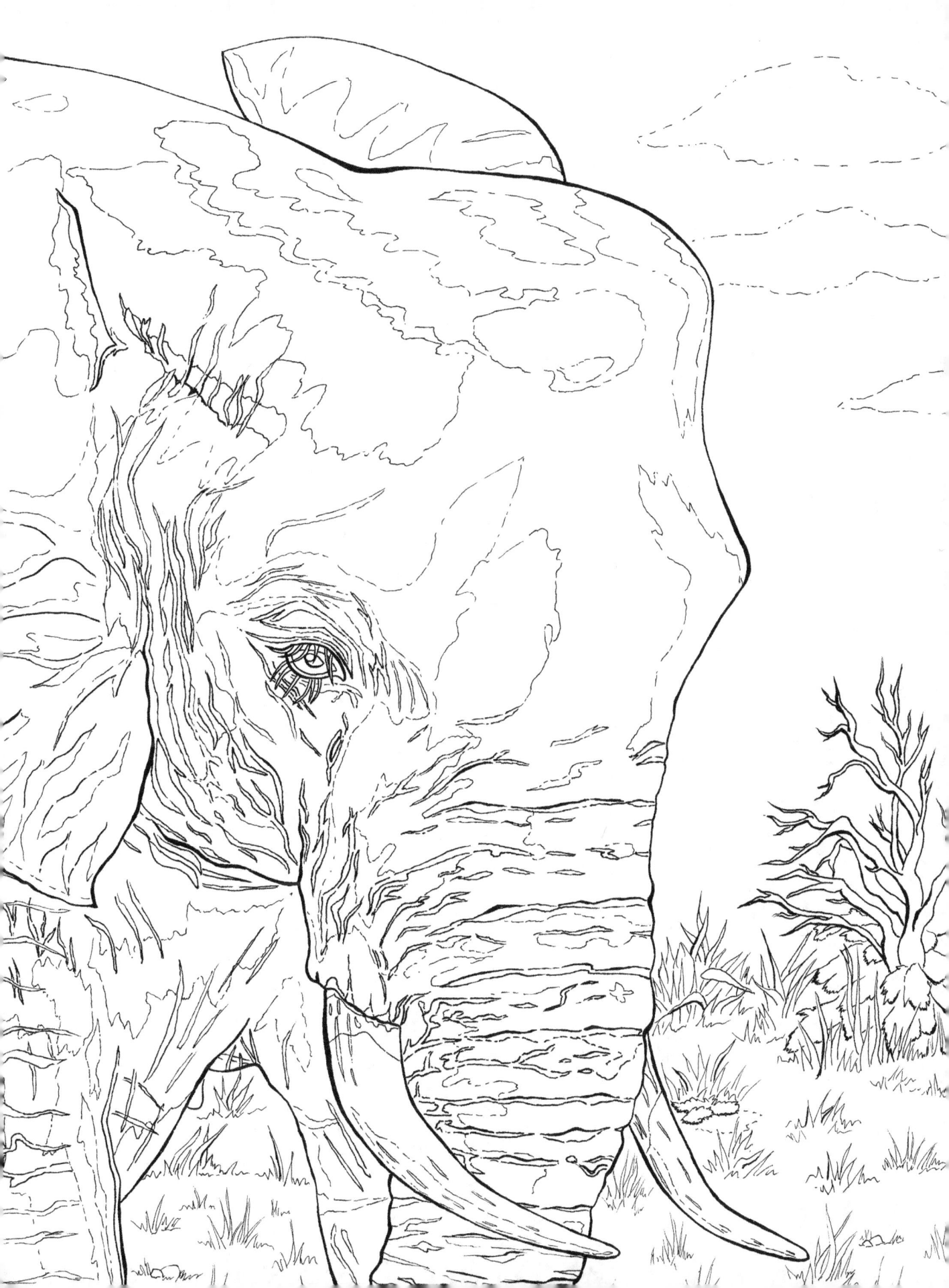

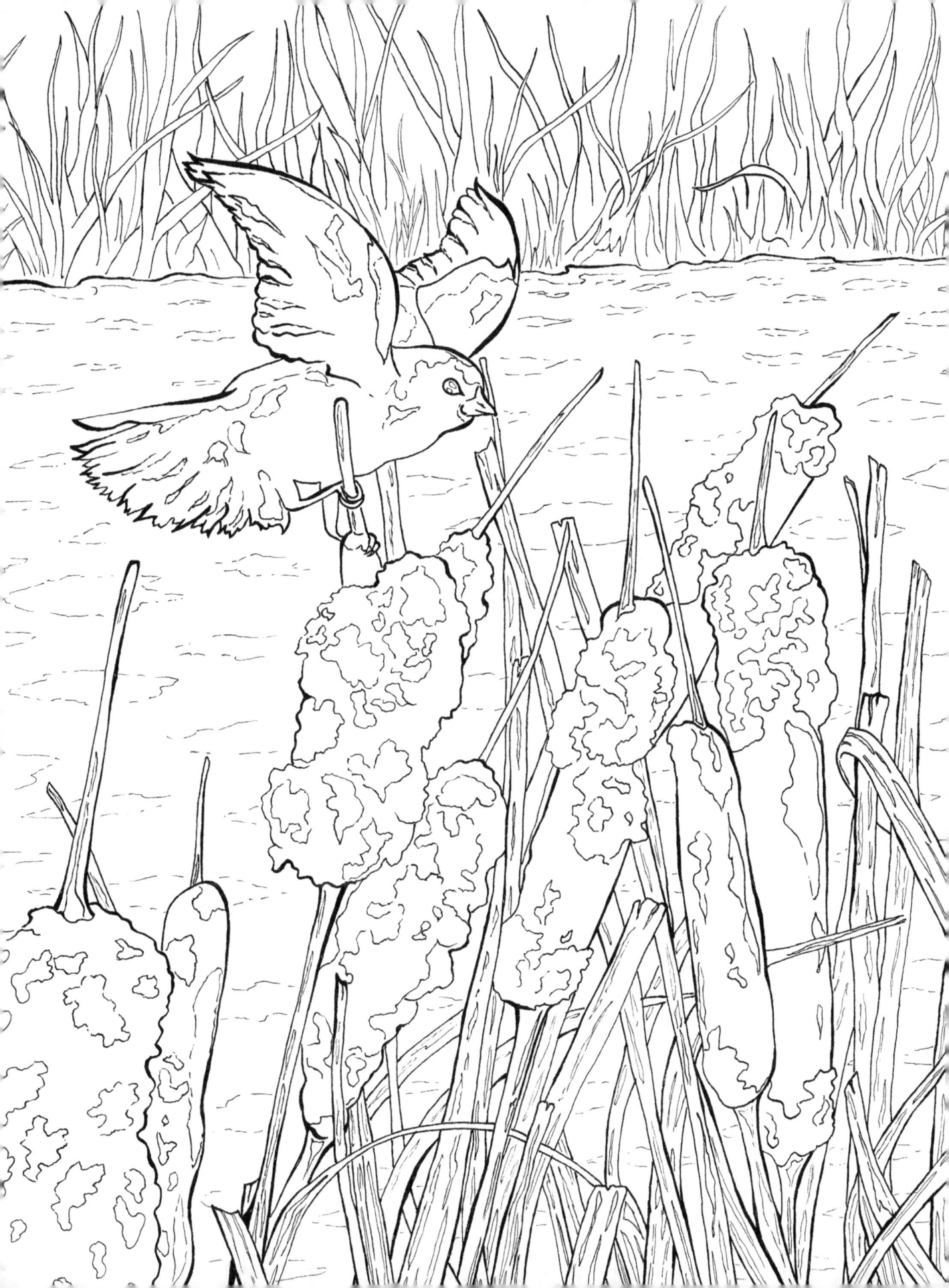

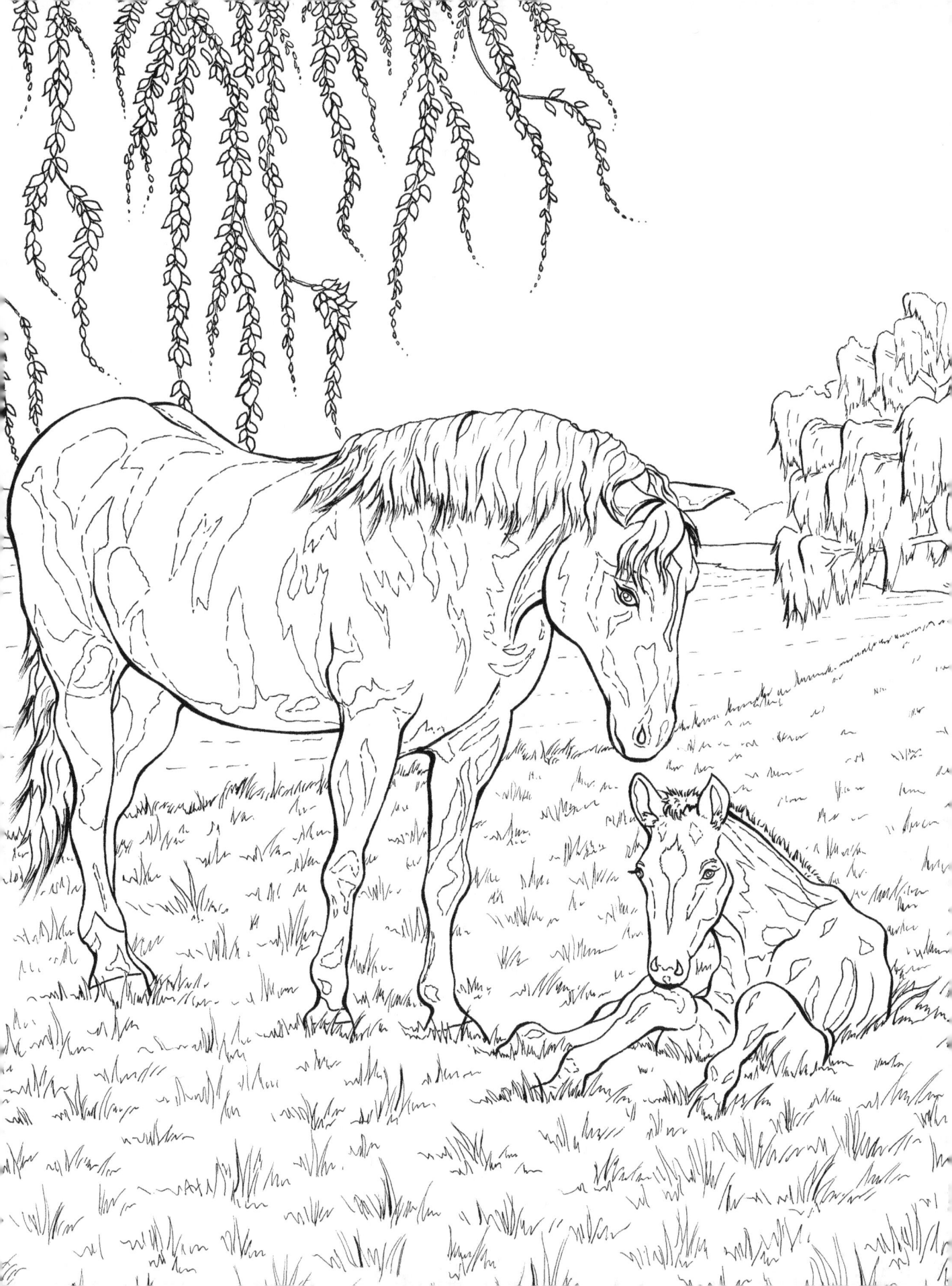

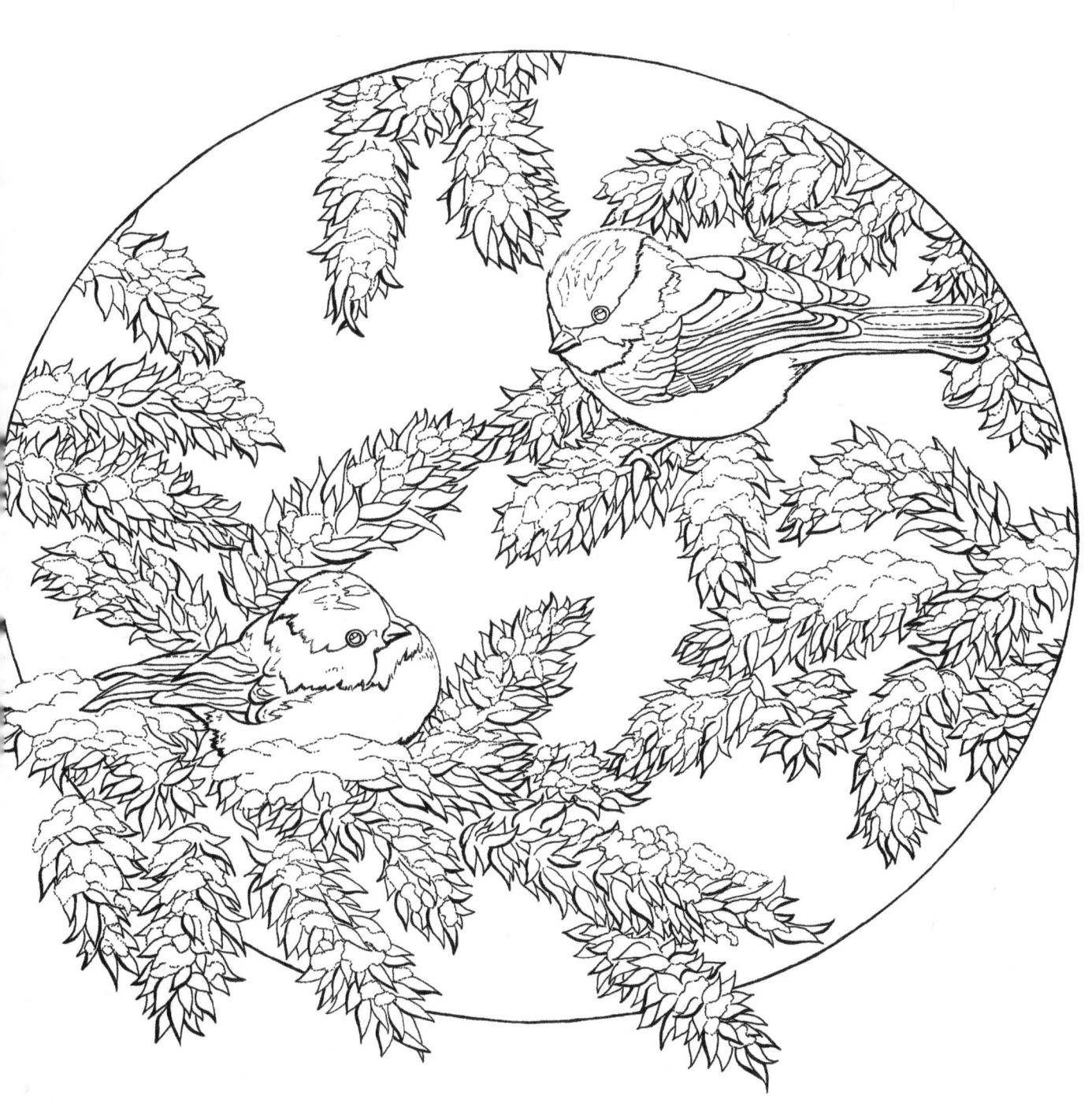

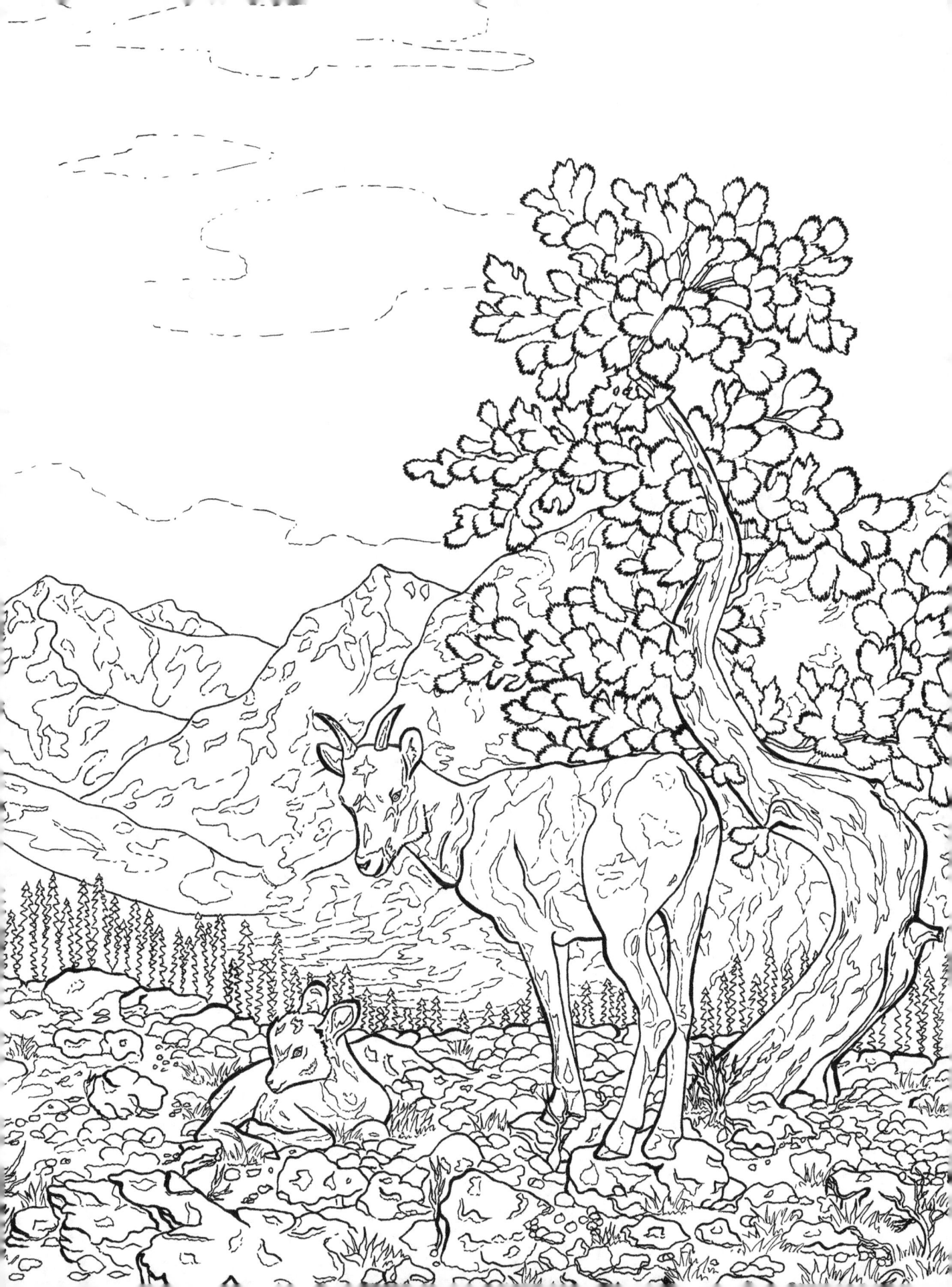

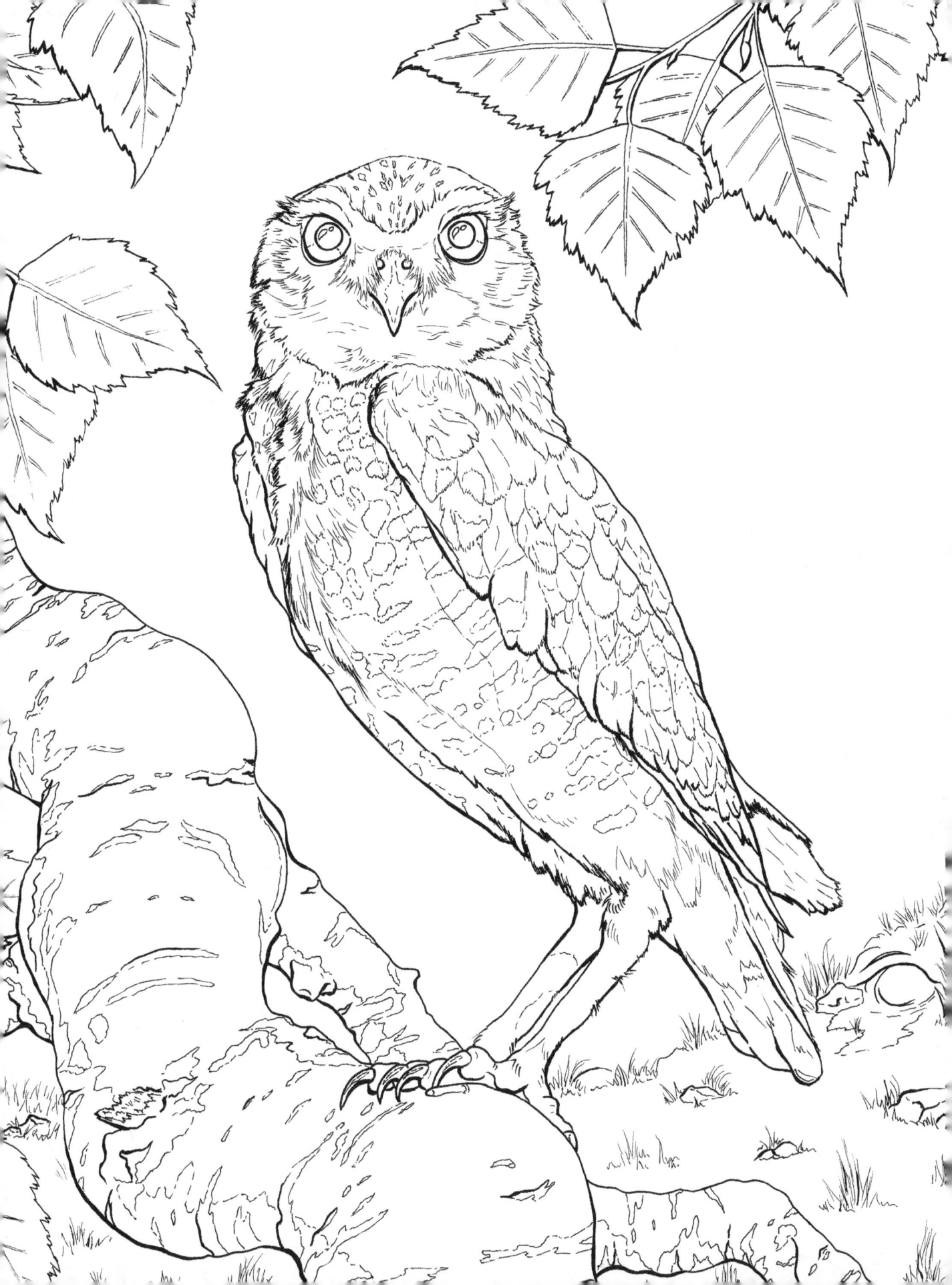

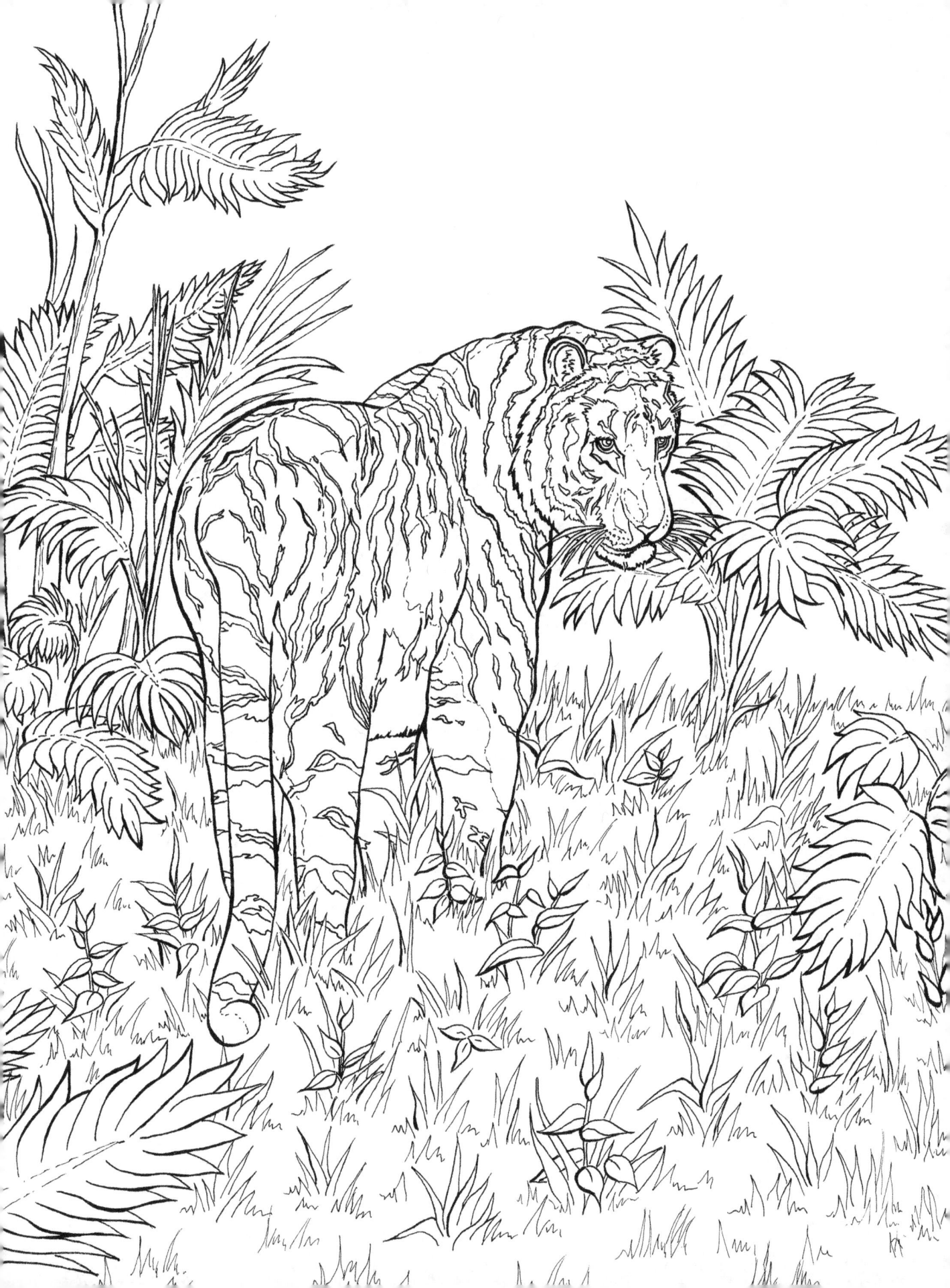

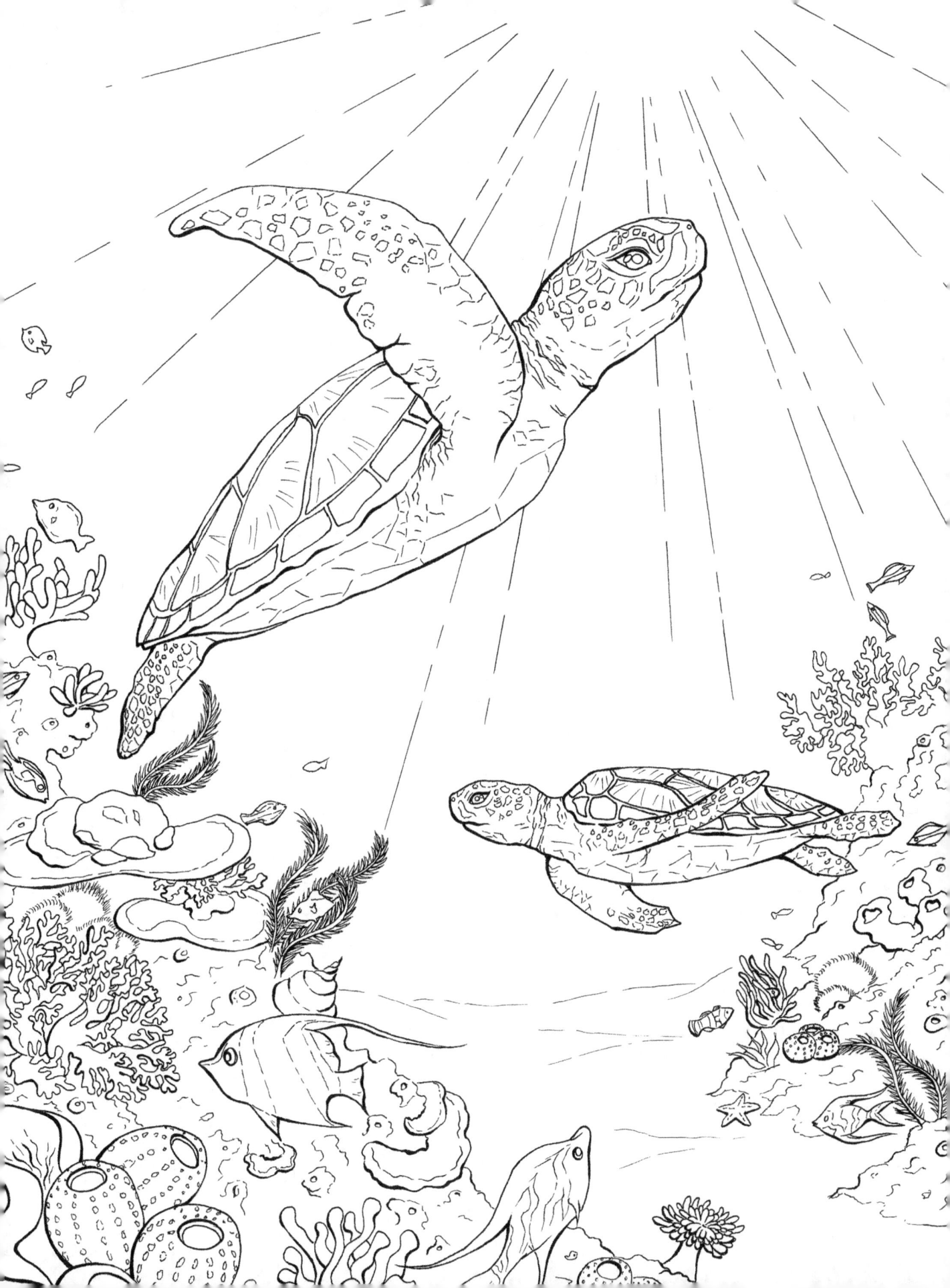

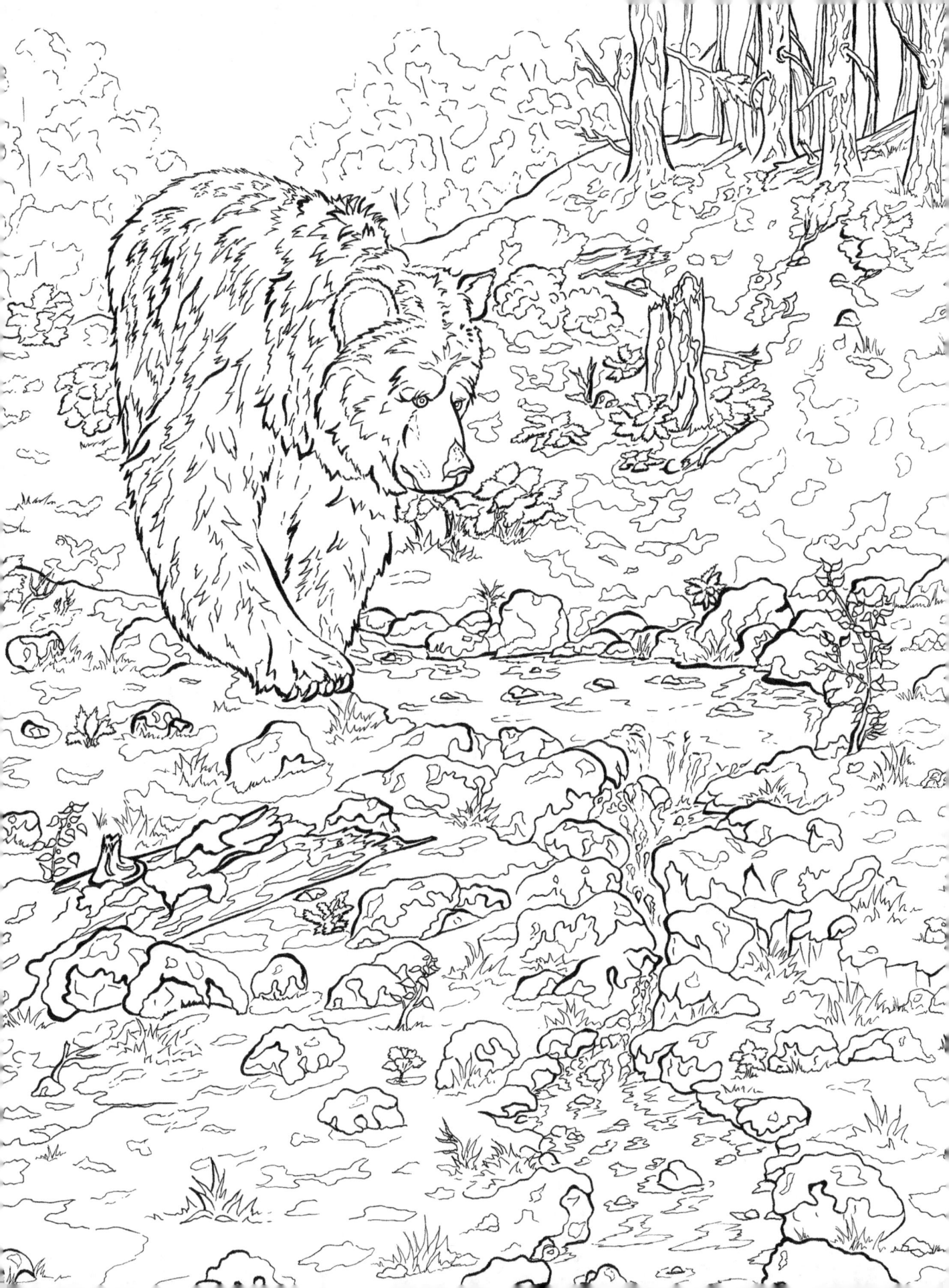

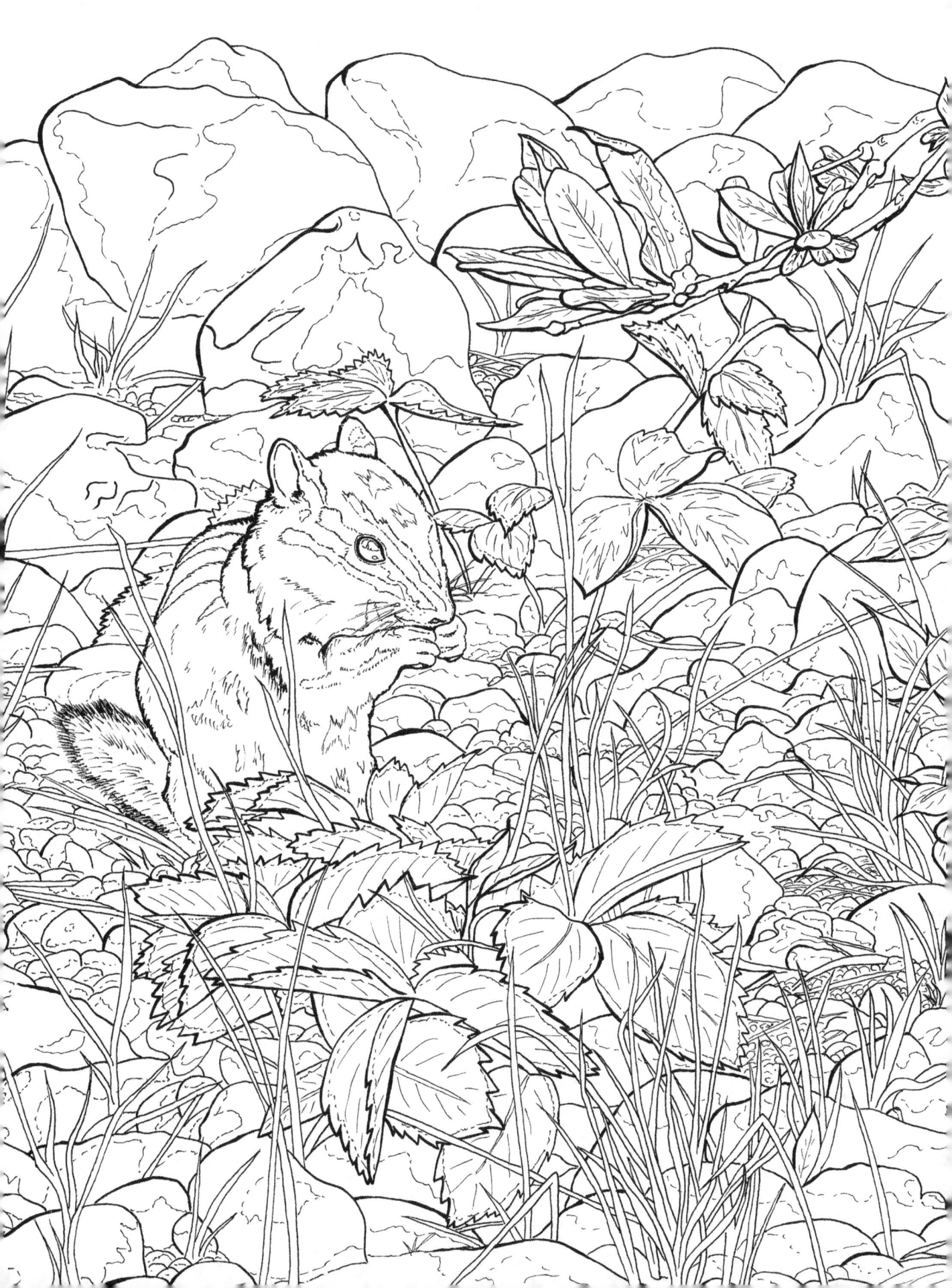

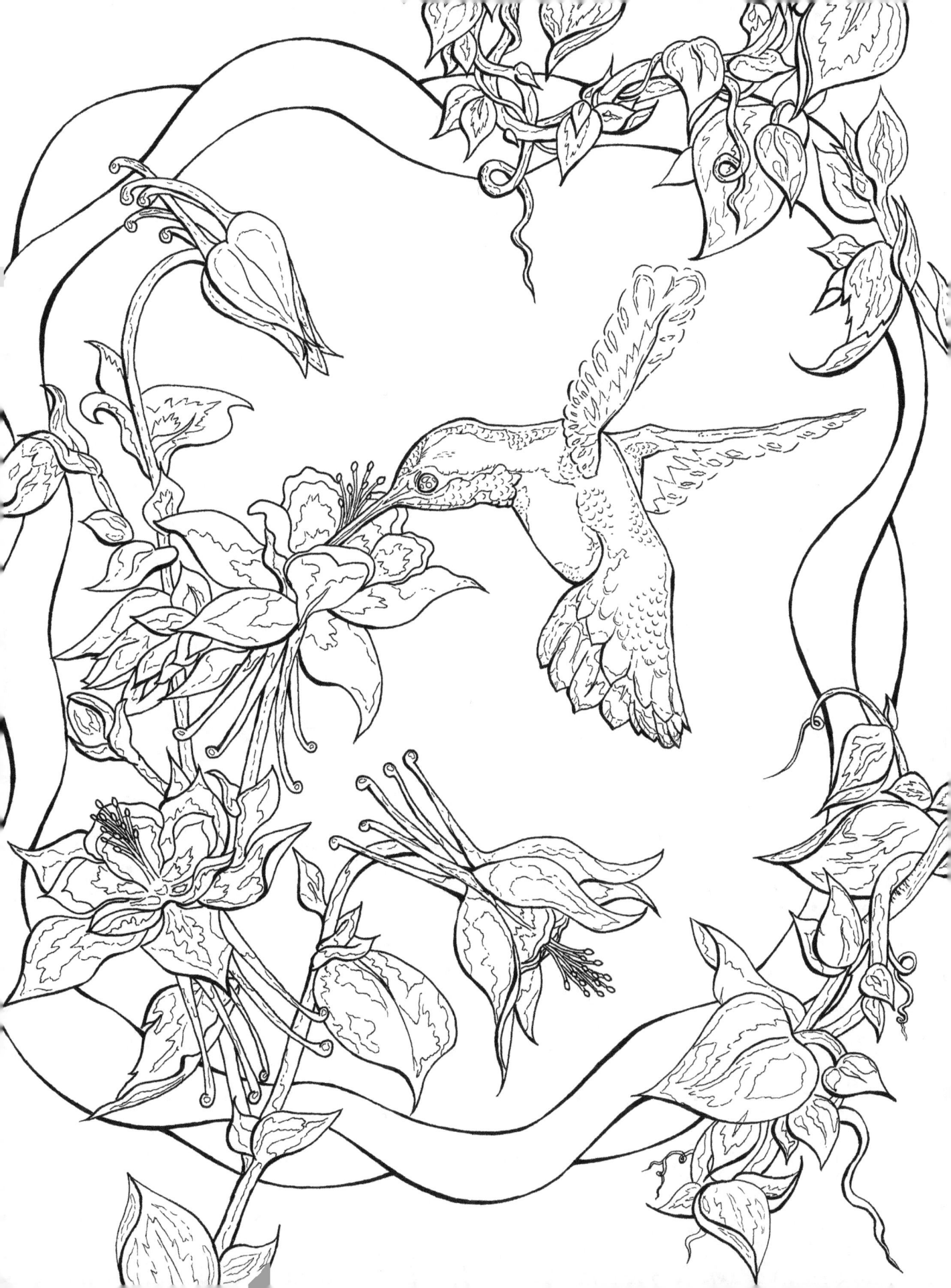

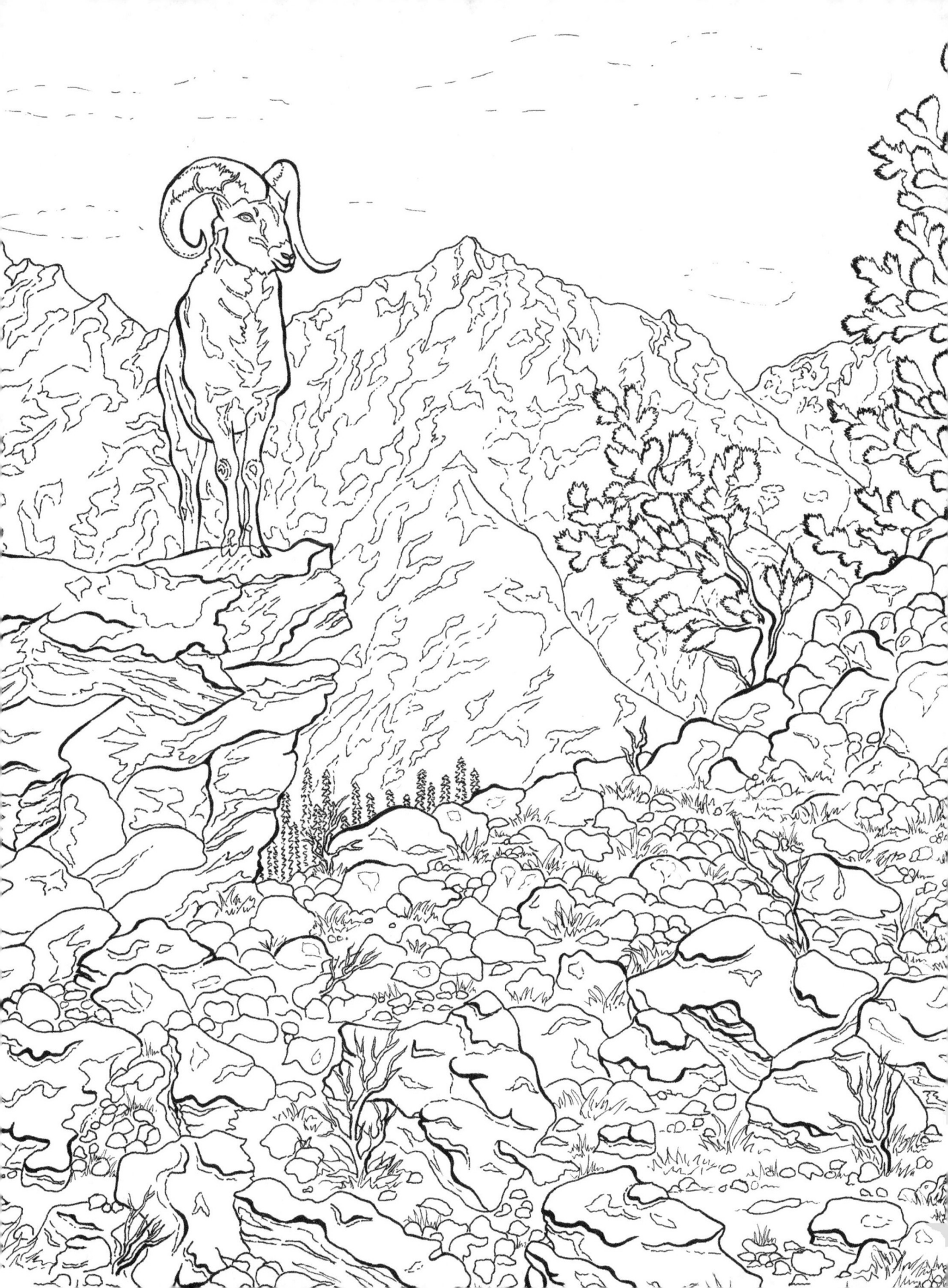

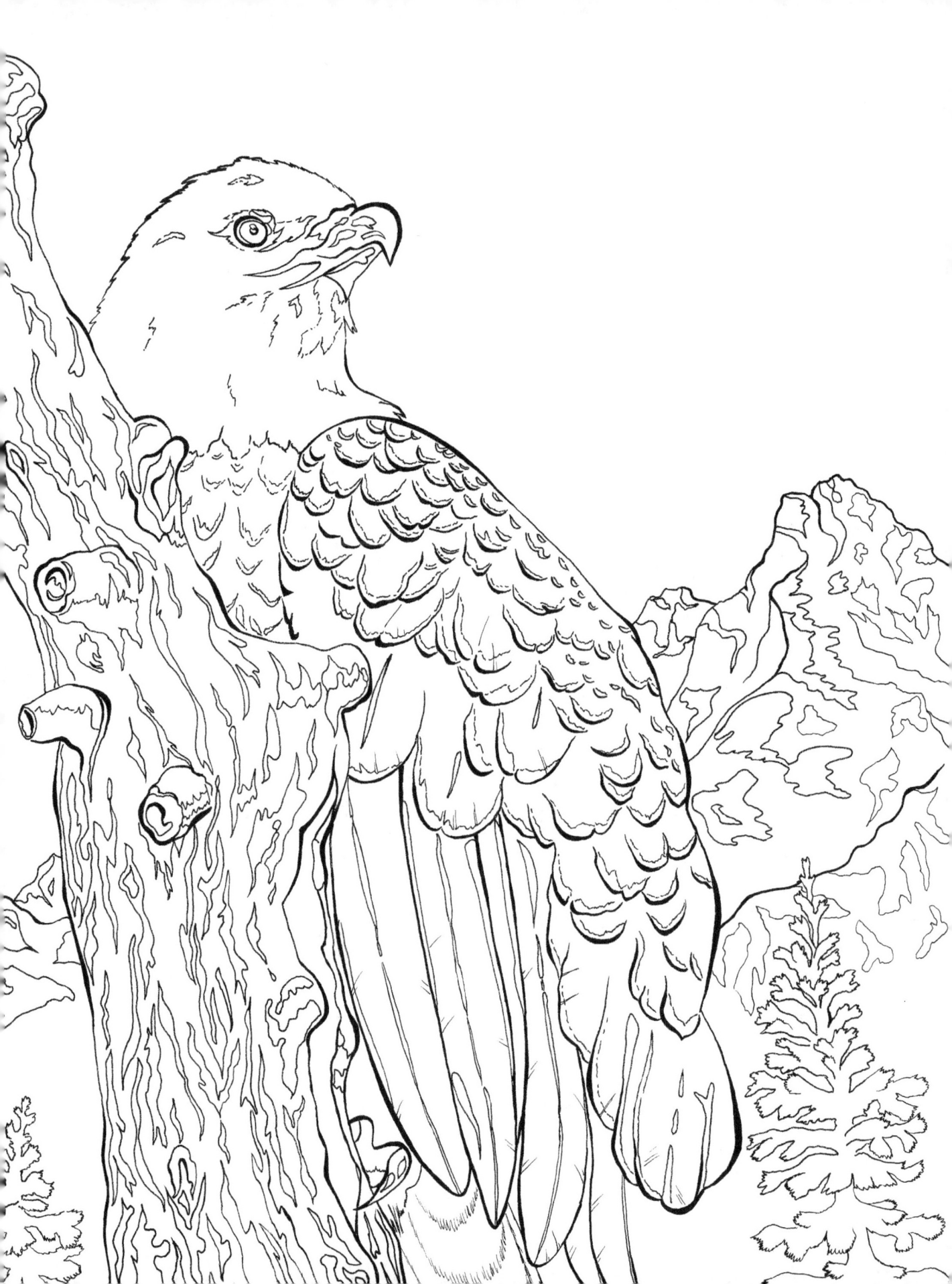

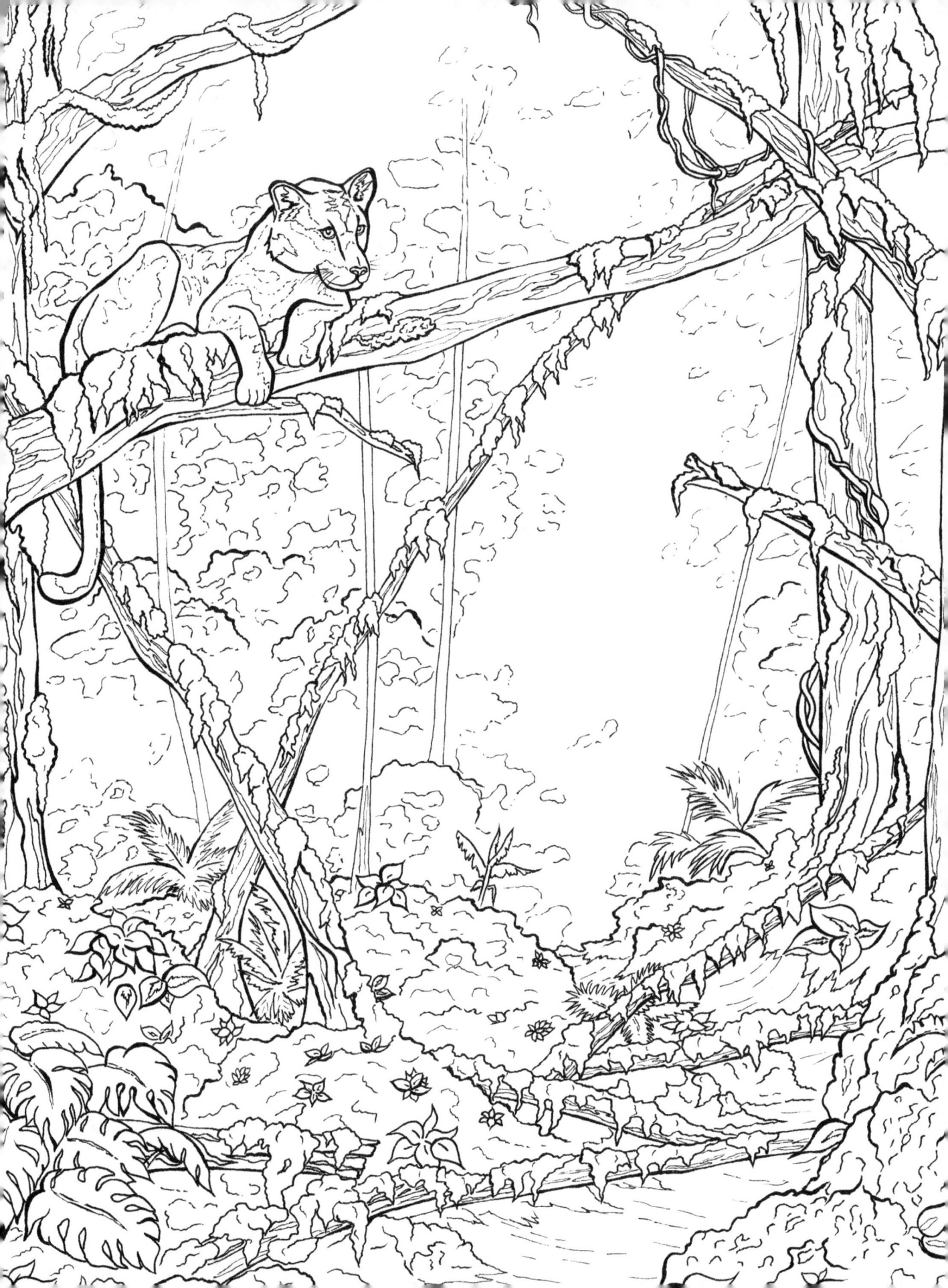

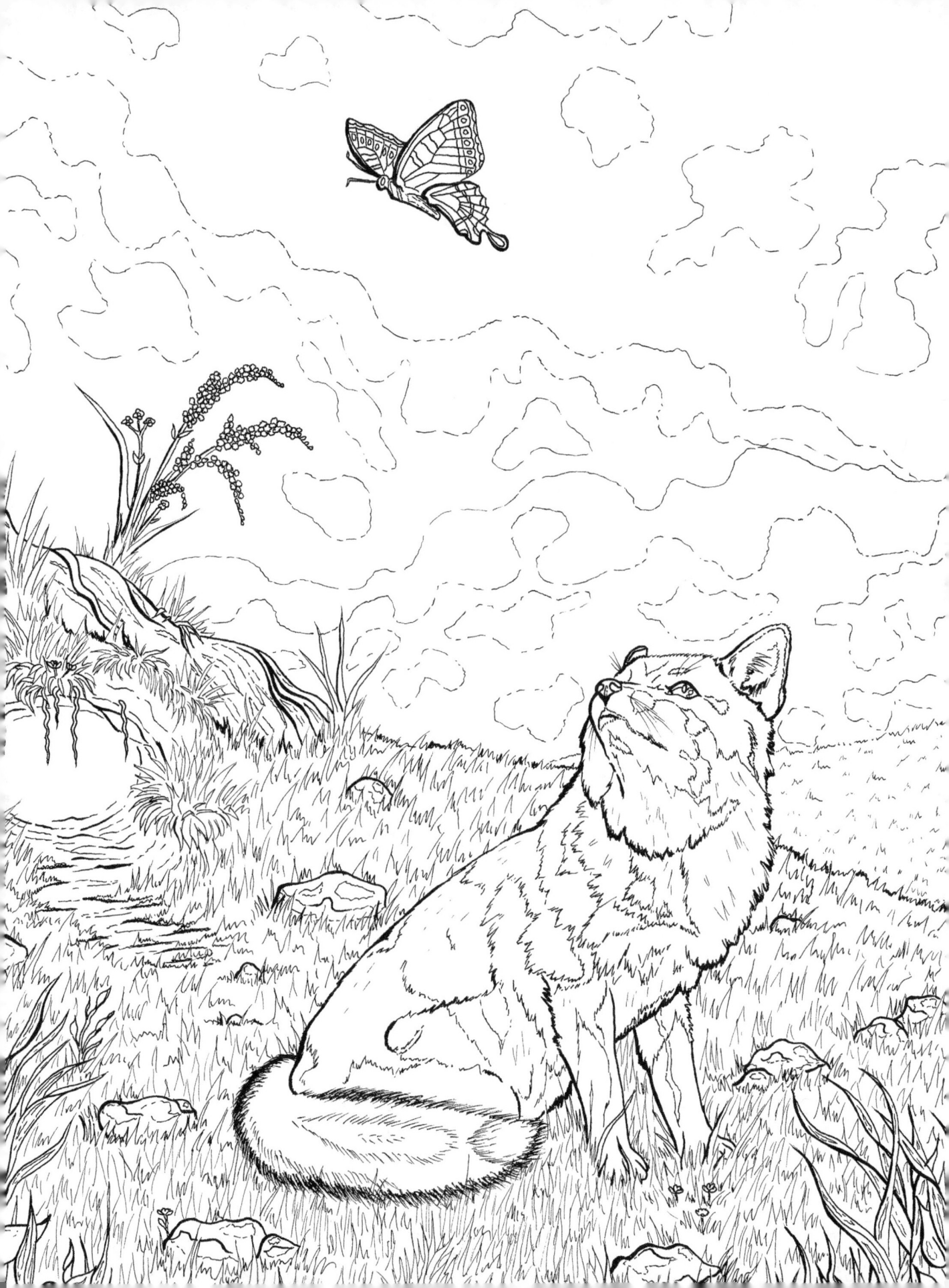

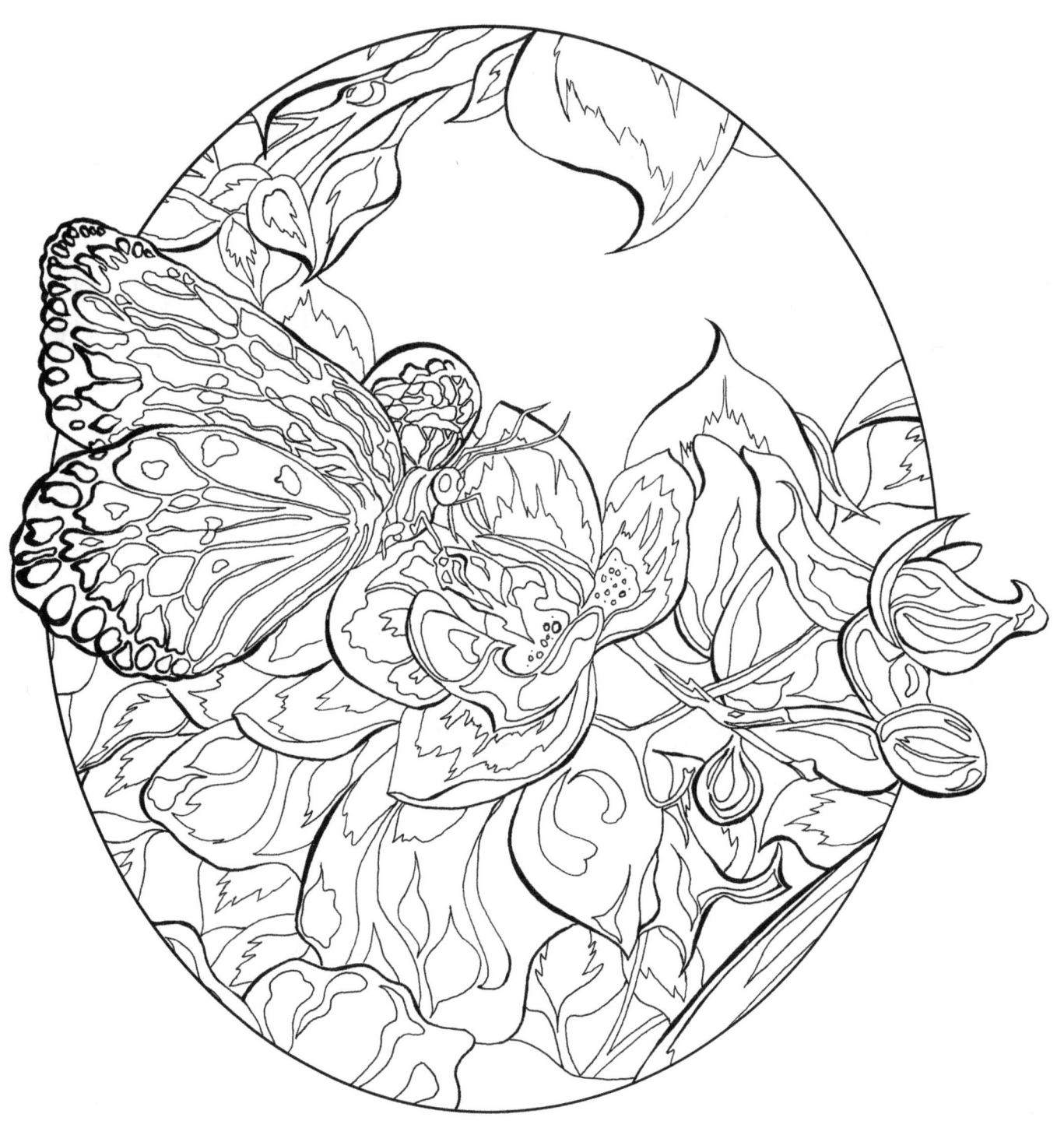

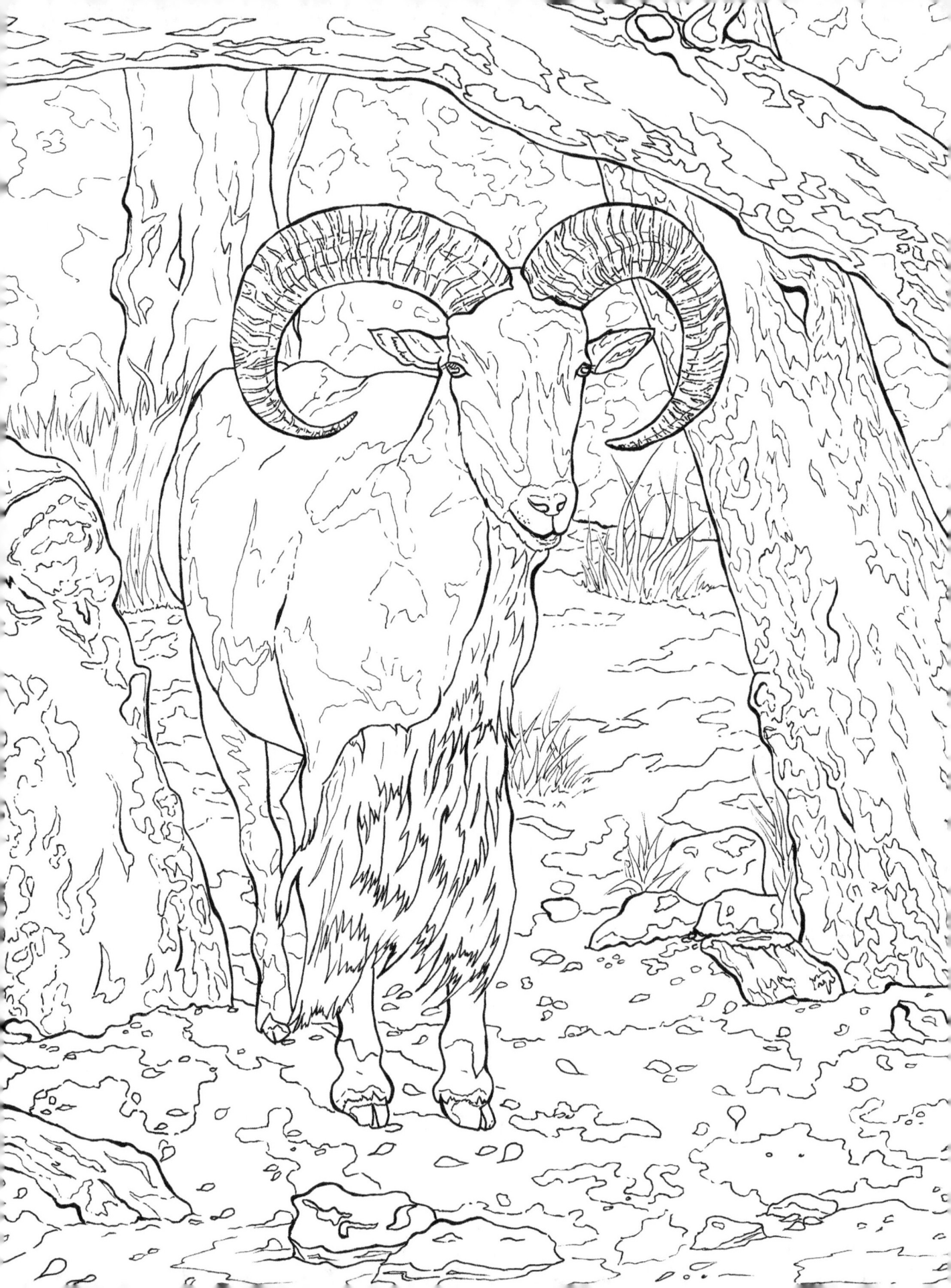

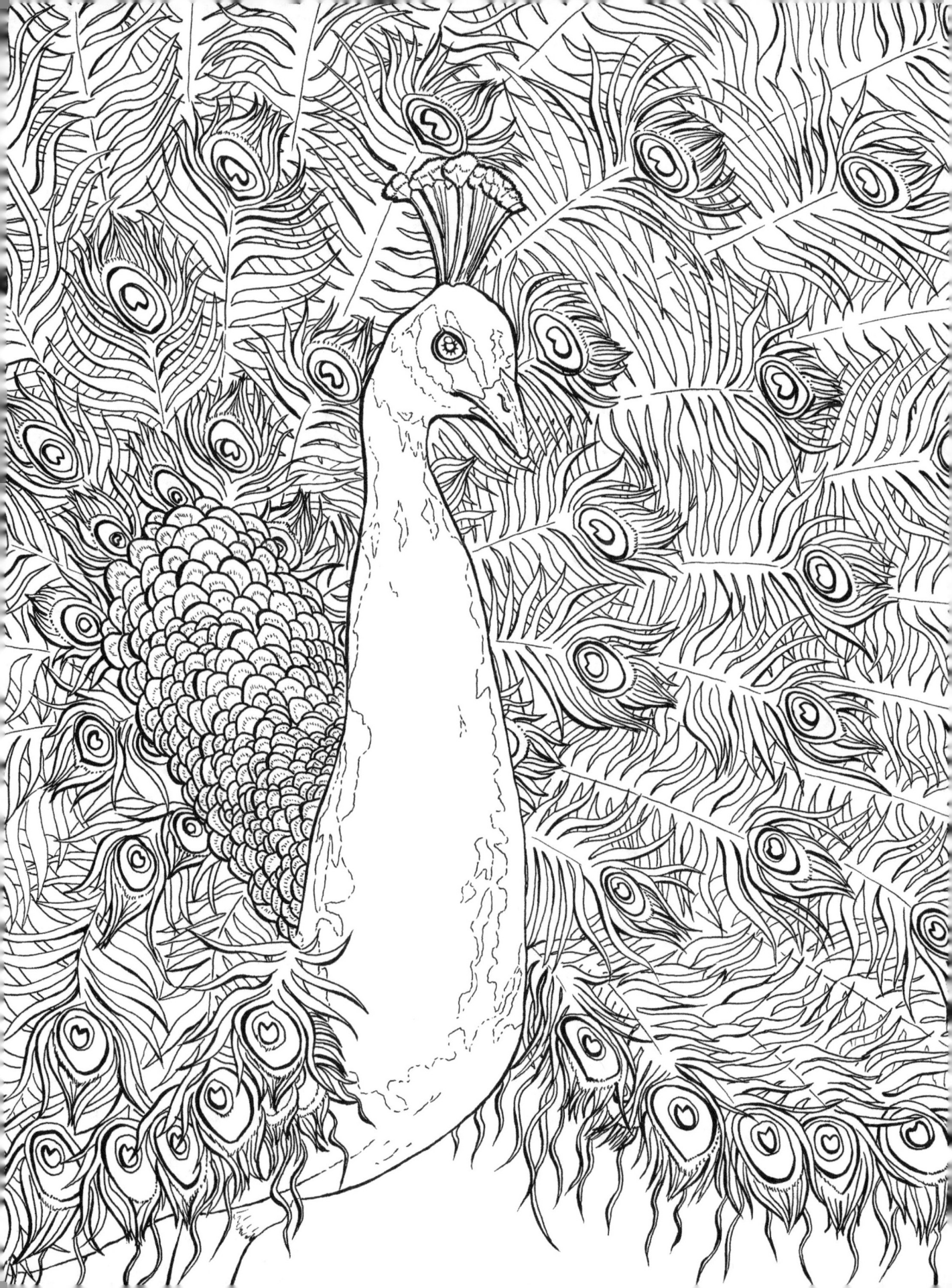

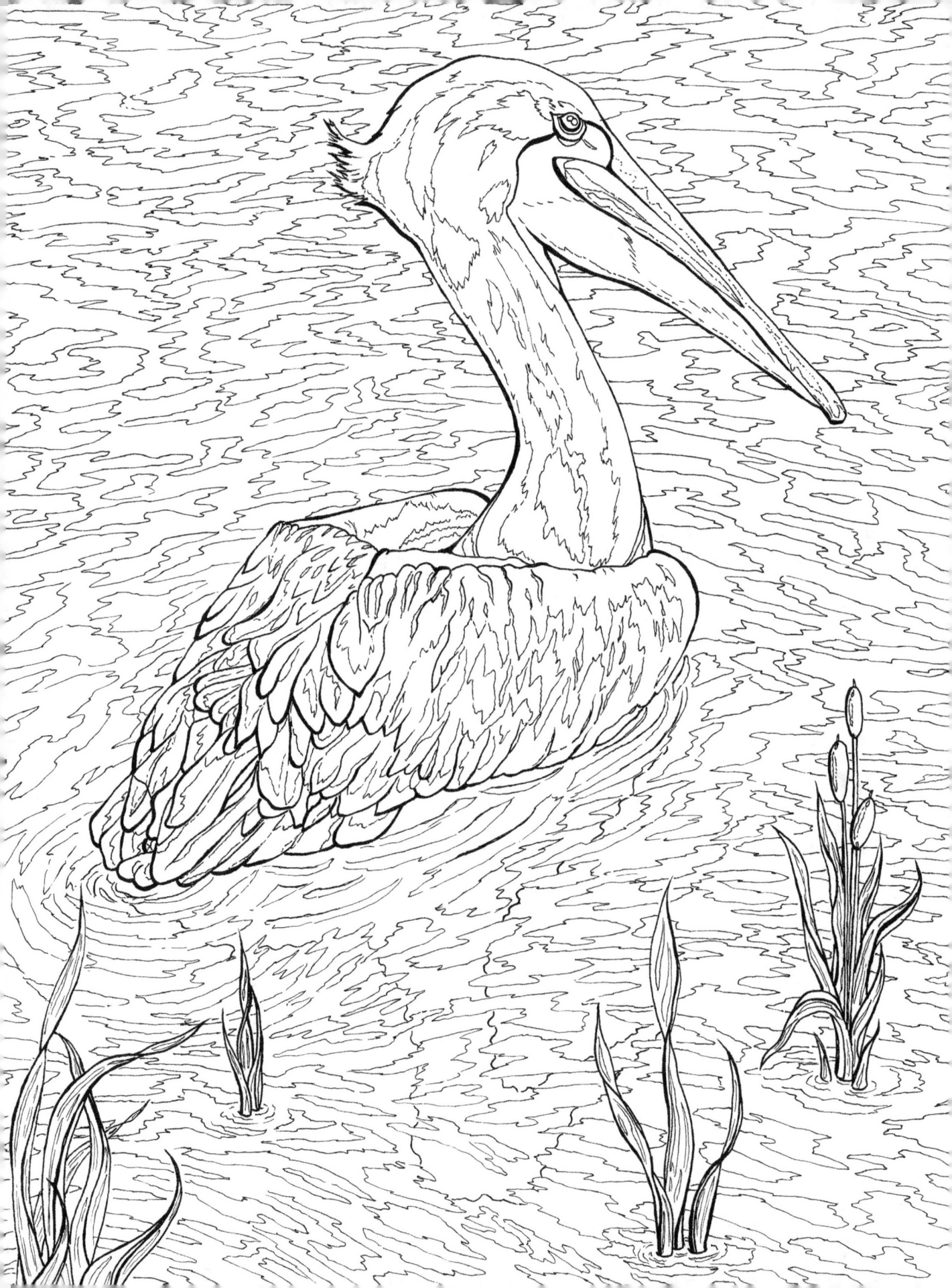

www.ingramcontent.com/pod-product-compliance
Lightning Source LLC
Chambersburg PA
CBHW062342220526
45469CB00008B/2801